*The lying-in room in Sara Ploos van Amstel's cabinet house, made in Holland in 1743 (see pages 14–16). As this was the room in which the new mother would receive her guests it had to be stylish and elegant. It has its own toilet and is finely decorated; the linen cupboard is full and silver miniatures are placed ostentatiously on the tables. (Gemeentemuseum, The Hague: photograph by N. Nicholson)*

# Dolls' Houses

## Halina Pasierbska

### A Shire book

Published in 2001 by Shire Publications Ltd,
Cromwell House, Church Street, Princes Risborough,
Buckinghamshire HP27 9AA, UK.
(Website: www.shirebooks.co.uk)

British Library Cataloguing in Publication Data:
Pasierbska, Halina
Dolls' houses. – 2nd ed. – (Shire album; 271)
1. Dollhouses 2. Dollhouses – History
I. Title 688.7'23'09
ISBN 0 7478 0501 6

Cover: *The Tate Baby House, an English dolls' house of c.1760, on display at the Bethnal Green Museum of Childhood.*

Back cover: *A tin house made by Louis Marx & Company (1920s to 1967) of the United States. (Faith Eaton Collection: photograph by John Gould)*

ACKNOWLEDGEMENTS

My special thanks to Faith Eaton, Leigh and Rachel Gotch of Bonhams and John Gould for the considerable help and support that they have given me. I would also like to thank the following for their kind help: Mark and Marjorie Allen Antiques; Bodo Hennig Puppenmobel GmbH; Brian Meade Agencies Ltd; Mrs S. Bulwer Long; Vina Cooke; the Dolls' House Emporium; Dr Michael Eisenhauer; Mattel UK Ltd; Rod Moore; Michal Morse; Nick Nicholson; the V&A Picture Library; Jane Williams.
The author and publishers acknowledge with gratitude those individuals and organisations who have kindly supplied photographs for this book and permitted their reproduction.

Printed in Malta by Gutenberg Press Limited, Gudja Road,
Tarxien PLA 19, Malta.

# Contents

*A small dolls' house dating from the late eighteenth century, in the Bethnal Green Museum of Childhood. (Courtesy of the V&A Picture Library)*

# Early German baby houses

The earliest recorded dolls' house was made in 1557–8 for Albert V, Duke of Bavaria. It was constructed and furnished as a copy of the prince's own residence and became popularly known as his Baby House or as the Munich House. Until the nineteenth century the terms 'baby house' and 'doll house' referred to the size of the house and not to its purpose.

Unfortunately the Munich House was burned down in 1614 but an inventory which had been compiled in 1598 by the Duke's councillor, Johann Baptist Fickler, survived. This document contains a detailed description of the size, structure and contents of the house, which must have been a perfect representation in miniature of a princely house of the period with its fine furnishings and fittings, reflecting the great wealth of its owner.

Enormously expensive, this impressive four-storey house required the skills of many craftsmen. No one guild specialised in the production of miniature objects and therefore often as many as fourteen guilds would have participated in the making and furnishing of one baby house.

Left and below: 'Mon Plaisir' ('My Pleasure') was an entire dolls' town consisting of over eighty rooms in glass-fronted boxes or cabinets like this one. It was made as a portrait of life in eighteenth-century Arnstadt, Germany, for a wealthy widow, Princess Augusta Dorothea of Schwarzburg-Arnstadt. This project became so expensive that she eventually ran out of money. The room shown in detail below is the Princess's salon. (Museen der Stadt, Arnstadt: photographs by N. Nicholson)

*The lying-in room
in 'Mon Plaisir'.
(Museen der Stadt,
Arnstadt:
photograph by N.
Nicholson)*

The textiles and furnishings were exquisite, made principally from silks and satins and decorated with gold embroidery. The bathroom was remarkably well equipped, containing bath tubs, washing bowls, copper tubs and such details as three bath hats hanging on the wall! The two kitchens contained all the appliances vital to their smooth running: pewter dishes, copper casseroles, implements of pewter, copper and brass, and chicken coops, which were a common and indispensable feature of kitchens of the time.

It would seem that the houses that followed served a serious instructional purpose as well as being objects which reflected the wealth of their owners. They were excellent visual aids which helped young girls of the privileged classes to learn, through

*A salon with a fine ceramic fireplace in
'Mon Plaisir'. (Museen der Stadt,
Arnstadt: photograph by N. Nicholson)*

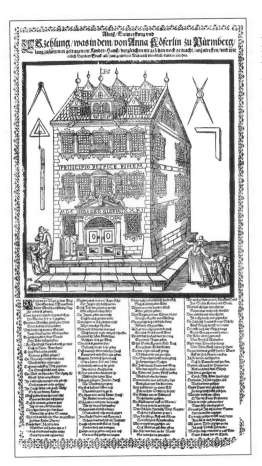

Abriſ/ Entwerffung end
Erʒehlung/ was in dem von Anna Köferlin ʒu Nürmberg/
lang ʒuſammen getragenem Kinder Hauß/ dergleichen nie geſehen noch gemacht/ anʒutreffen/ vnd wie
etlich Hundert Stuck/ alle ʒum gemeinen Nuz auch dienſtlich/ darinn juſtehen.

PRINCIPIO PRESPICE FINEM

MDC SOLI DEO GLORIA XXXI

play, how to become good household managers. In 1765 Paul Stetten, the Younger, a historian living at Augsburg, wrote in his *Commentary of the Copper Engravings Showing Scenes from the History of the City of Augsburg*: 'Concerning the training of maidens, I must make reference to the playthings many of them played with until they were brides, namely the so-called Baby Houses. These contained everything that was needed for house and home, presented in miniature, and some went so far in lavishness that such a plaything came to be worth something like a thousand guilders or more.'

Another very interesting house, for which unfortunately only the woodcut broadsheet survives, dates from 1631 and was clearly intended for the instruction of young women in their household duties. It was an unusual project in that it was inspired by a lady, Anna Köferlin, who had it built despite her lack of financial resources and displayed it upon payment of an admission charge. The house was very large, measuring 240 cm (7 feet $10^1/2$ inches) in height, 134 cm (4 feet $4^3/4$ inches) in width and approximately 100 cm (3 feet $3^1/4$ inches) in depth, and represented a house typical of the

*Reproduction of the broadsheet which accompanied Anna Köferlin's House of 1631. (Photograph by N. Nicholson)*

Nuremberg style of the period with a steep roof and bottle-glass windows. The message from Anna Köferlin in the broadsheet clearly emphasises the value of hard work and good domestic organisation:

So look you then at this Baby House, ye babes, inside and out. Look at it and learn well ahead how you shall live in days to come. See how all is arranged, in kitchen, parlour and chamber, and yet is also well adorned. See what great number of chattels a well arrayed house does need. But at times one may also manage well with little, if one be content. Look all around you, look behind you, look everywhere, how much there has been put on show for you, hundreds of pieces. Of bedding, of handsome presses, of pewter, copper and brass, fitted up in such a way that though so small, yet everything may well be put to general use...

Four outstanding houses are shown today in the Germanisches Nationalmuseum in Nuremberg: one dating from 1611; another, known as the Stromer House, from 1639; one from the later seventeenth century, loaned by the Bäumler family; and a slightly larger one that belonged to the Kress von Kressenstein family. These are all tall houses of three or four storeys, closely resembling Anna Köferlin's House. The kitchen and the living room, usually known as the 'best' or 'state' room, tended to be located on an upper floor whilst storage, stables and maids' rooms were to be found in the basement or cellar.

The 1611 house is a particularly handsome one. Amongst its many interesting features is a painting on the cellar door of a maid leading an undressed child to the bathroom. Both wear bath hats and the maid carries a tub under her arm. Bathing, though not necessarily common, was an important part of the routine of most upper-middle-class Nuremberg families. The great hall of this house is decorated with pictures of a merry group of people sitting round a table in a garden. Paintings such as these often served as cheap substitutes for wall hangings and tapestries.

Above: *The Kress House, dating from the seventeenth century, formerly in the Kress von Kressenstein family. (Germanisches Nationalmuseum: photograph by N. Nicholson)*

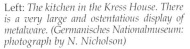

Left: *The kitchen in the Kress House. There is a very large and ostentatious display of metalware. (Germanisches Nationalmuseum: photograph by N. Nicholson)*

7

Above left: *The merchant's trading room in the Bäumler House in the Germanisches Nationalmuseum, Nuremberg. (Photograph by John Gould)*

Above right: *The great hall in the 1611 house in the Germanisches Nationalmuseum, seen from the garden. Note the display of pewter along the wall. This is an unusual feature in a baby house. (Photograph by John Gould)*

Left: *An exterior view of the 1611 house. Note the kitchen on the first floor and the garden in the basement, next to the great hall. (Germanisches Nationalmuseum: photograph by N. Nicholson)*

The Stromer House is notable for its well stocked kitchen and cellar, which contains a stable. It also contains a linen press, which may be seen on the first floor. Linen, cut or uncut, was stored folded flat in large cupboards, it being usual to keep lengths of cloth for future use. Examples of these pieces of cloth can still be seen today in baby houses, stored in exactly the same way as they were then.

*The bedroom on the first floor of the Stromer House, 1639. Note the wood panelling and the ceramic stove. (Germanisches Nationalmuseum: photograph by N. Nicholson)*

Two special features of the Bäumler House are the bottle-glass windows at each side (most of the windows of baby houses had wooden shutters or imitation glass windows made of paper or thin sheets of talc) and a merchant's shop neatly stocked with groceries, medicines and paper. This feature was typical of Nuremberg life, for it was usual for a trader to live and to conduct his business on the same premises.

The main attraction of the Kress House is the beautifully carved, original balustrades. Those of the other houses were unfortunately lost or replaced.

The Bethnal Green Museum of Childhood in London displays the only example of an early German house outside Germany or Austria. Dated 1673, it is considerably smaller than the ones at Nuremberg; it consists of only four rooms but is furnished with the same attention to detail and has a clearly visible privy!

These early German houses reflect the standard of comfort in which the well-to-do lived in the sixteenth and seventeenth centuries and the emphasis that was placed on efficient household management.

*The Nuremberg House, 1673, now in the Bethnal Green Museum of Childhood. The metal stars were a feature of Nuremberg architecture until they were banned in the early eighteenth century because of their tendency to fall in high winds, posing a considerable safety hazard. (Courtesy of the V&A Picture Library)*

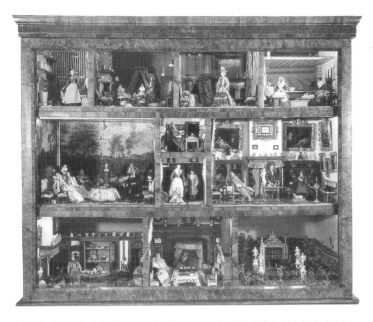

*Petronella de la Court's cabinet house from the seventeenth century, in the Centraal Museum, Utrecht. (Photograph by N. Nicholson)*

# The Dutch cabinet house

The practical beauty of the German houses with their educational overtones contrasts with the elegant sophistication of the Dutch cabinet houses of the seventeenth and eighteenth centuries. The most striking difference is architectural, for the German houses tended to resemble buildings but the Dutch were usually housed in pieces of furniture like those used for storing linen or china. That was why they came to be known as cabinet houses.

As a result of Holland's expanding trade with Asia and the New World there had grown up a prosperous class of bankers and merchants who were eager to display evidence of their success by collecting precious or interesting items in 'cabinets of curiosities'. Amongst the coins and gems small copies of domestic items in gold or silver took pride of place. Collecting these miniatures became such a passion that whole households were reproduced. Intended as adults' playthings, these treasured collections were displayed as symbols of the owner's wealth and social standing.

Perhaps the best-known of these houses is the one that was made for Petronella de la Court in Amsterdam and is now at the Centraal Museum at Utrecht. It was started between 1674 and 1690 and is thus also one of the oldest. It has a complicated but well documented history. A guide-catalogue of its contents compiled by Margareta, daughter of Pieter van der Beek, who owned the house after 1754, survives and the contents have been

*Detail from the music room in the Petronella de la Court cabinet house in the Centraal Museum, Utrecht. (Photograph by N. Nicholson)*

displayed as she described them. It has several fine rooms, the most striking being two on the middle level: the 'art' or 'curiosity' room, and the salon, where musical pastimes were pursued. The walls and ceiling of the salon are covered with large paintings by Frederick de Moucheron (1633–86). Both rooms are filled with precious works of art, including paintings, engravings, porcelain, ivory and coins, most of which were specially commissioned by their owners, as in the other Dutch cabinets.

Another feature that they all had in common was the 'lying-in' room, in which a new mother would receive her guests. Whilst the nursery was usually located in the attic or basement, this

*The lying-in room in the Petronella de la Court cabinet house in the Centraal Museum, Utrecht. (Photograph by N. Nicholson)*

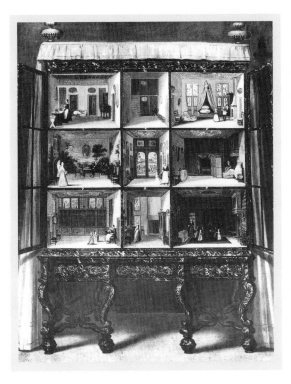

room was expected to reflect the social status of its mistress and would be appropriately furnished. Tea, coffee and chocolate were new beverages at this time and it is usual for this room to contain facilities for such refreshments. It would also have a well stocked and prominent linen cupboard. As the washing was done only about once a year it was important to be seen to own a plentiful supply of linen.

The Rijksmuseum in Amsterdam possesses two beautiful cabinet houses. One is believed to have been the much loved property of Petronella Dunois, who brought it as part of her dowry to her marriage in 1677. The cabinet and stand are made of walnut, and a pincushion in the house is dated 1676, when it is thought that she furnished the house. Unlike their more prominently placed German counterparts, the kitchens of the cabinet houses were usually located in the basement. The kitchen in this house, like the one in that of Petronella de la Court, has a privy in the corner and the toilet utensils are unhygienically suspended over the cooking pots.

The other house is one made for Petronella Oortman (daughter of Petronella de la Court) in the latter half of the seventeenth century. An early-eighteenth-century painting of the house by Jacob Appel survives and is chiefly useful as a document of the fashion of the times since much that has been depicted in it does not survive. The rooms are numbered, which suggests that the

13

*The laundry room in Sara Ploos van Amstel's cabinet house contains a linen press on the left. On the table is a cane cone upon which nightcaps were placed in order to retain their shape. (Gemeentemuseum, The Hague: photograph by N. Nicholson)*

house may have been displayed at some time.

A striking feature of this house is its 'best' kitchen, where the housewife displayed the collection of china which formed part of her dowry. It was used more as a sitting room than for the preparation of food, which was done in the adjoining kitchen. Of all the cabinet houses, this one probably contains the most superb collection of miniature items, including ivory and rosewood furniture and several pieces of silver made by the craftsman Christian Waarenburg.

In the Gemeentemuseum in The Hague is a huge walnut cabinet house made in 1743 by Jan Meijjer for Sara Ploos van Amstel, who furnished it with the contents and rooms of three seventeenth-century cabinet houses which she had bought at auction earlier in that year. The destruction of these houses, which were unfortunately not described, is regrettable, but the owner kept a precise record of all the changes made and the names of all the craftsmen involved.

*A view of the collector's room or curio room in Sara Ploos van Amstel's cabinet house. The wall cabinet contains coins and shells, and close by may be seen part of a chaise longue covered in patterned cloth of the type that was fashionable in the late seventeenth century. (Gemeentemuseum, The Hague: photograph by N. Nicholson)*

The music room in Sara Ploos van Amstel's cabinet house. The dolls were specially made but most of the small brass, silver and glass items came from the three older cabinets which she had taken apart to make this new one. Note the cabinet of curiosities against the wall at the back and also the silver sconces on the wall. (Gemeentemuseum, The Hague: photograph by N. Nicholson)

The courtyard in Sara Ploos van Amstel's cabinet house. The walls are decorated with views of formal gardens. (Gemeentemuseum, The Hague: photograph by N. Nicholson)

The kitchen in Sara Ploos van Amstel's cabinet house. The walls are finely decorated but the showpieces here are the items of kitchenware which are on display. (Gemeentemuseum, The Hague: photograph by N. Nicholson)

*The porcelain room, a miniature example of a wealthy Dutch collector's room, in Sara Ploos van Amstel's house. (Gemeentemuseum, The Hague: photograph by N. Nicholson)*

Two rooms in this cabinet are so magnificent that they would have been the envy of any wealthy Dutchman. The porcelain room has a resplendent display of blue and white 'china' (actually painted glass) whilst in the music room stand a harpsichord, a viola da gamba and some splendid Dutch seventeenth-century glasses used for refreshments for the musicians.

The Dutch cabinet house was important to its owner principally as a symbol of wealth and social standing. The cabinet style was little imitated elsewhere, although in Great Britain the Westbrook Baby House (1705) is in the Dutch style, as is the later John Egerton Killer cabinet (1830s) in the collection at the Bethnal Green Museum of Childhood.

# The English baby house in the eighteenth century

The earliest English baby houses were evidently more closely influenced by the Dutch than the German style. Many surviving early examples resemble furnished cabinets or cupboards with or without legs or stands. An English tradition gradually emerged and cabinets and cupboards evolved into miniature buildings. Some were supported by an arched base, such as the house at Uppark and the King's Lynn Baby House; some had substantial bases; and others were supported by elegant or simple stands. Most of the contents were made by craftsmen specialising in reproducing miniatures and there were silver utensils of every kind made by silversmith toymen. At first these items were imported from Holland, where they had been made for some time. In England they were not freely available until after the restoration of the monarchy in 1660.

Several examples of baby houses survive but only a few retain their original appearance and furnishings. The best-known houses are Ann Sharp's Baby House, Nostell Priory Baby House, Uppark Baby House, the Blackett Baby House and the Tate Baby House.

The oldest known English dolls' house is the privately owned Ann Sharp's House. It was given to Ann Sharp in the late seventeenth century by her godmother, the future Queen Anne of England. Despite its royal connection, the house lacks the elegant craftsmanship evident in later houses. It combines the simplicity of structure of a Nuremberg house with informality in its presentation. The contents are not uniform in quality, so that some fine items, such as the beautiful embroidered green silk hangings, an alabaster tea service and pieces of seventeenth-century miniature silver, mingle with cruder objects, such as a portrait of Queen Anne painted on the back of a playing card.

Pinned to the clothing of the dolls, some of wax, some of wood, are labels indicating who they are: 'Roger, ye butler' is to be found by the hall table whilst 'Sarah Gill, ye child's maid' stands in the nursery. Also in the nursery is a paper dolls' house with miniature paper furniture. A curious feature in the boudoir is the wax relief portrait of a fifteenth-century witch, Mother Skipton.

More elegant is the Uppark Baby House (1730–40), now owned by the National Trust. Sara Lethieullier, who owned it then, brought it to Uppark in West Sussex when she married Sir Matthew Fetherstonhaugh in 1747. It is three storeys high and stands on an arched base. It bears the coat of arms of Christopher

*This cupboard house made from oak dates from the late seventeenth century to the early eighteenth century. It is an oak cupboard with four rooms, each with a fireplace in the corner. The room on the first floor has a panel above the fireplace for a picture. This early style was influenced by the Dutch custom of using cupboards as houses and this house would probably have been furnished with items of very fine workmanship. (Mark and Marjorie Allen Antiques: photograph courtesy of Bonhams)*

17

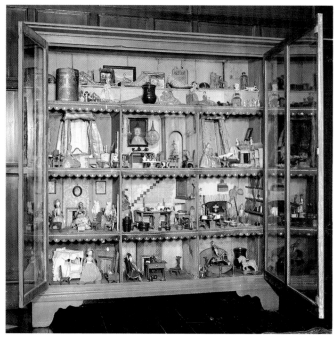

*The interior of Ann Sharp's Baby House, which dates from the end of the seventeenth century. This is the oldest known English baby house. It is interesting because it is a very early example of a cupboard house, which was a Dutch tradition, and also because it was meant to be played with by a little girl: most early houses were principally adults' toys. (Private collection: photograph by N. Nicholson)*

Lethieullier on the pediment.

The nine-roomed house is painted white and bears a row of figures on the roof which, together with the pillars that support the house, gives it a classical appearance. A well equipped kitchen can be seen in the basement. The dining room is on the first floor, reflecting the trend in eighteenth-century England for the family to separate its activities from those of the servants. Formerly it was usual for the mistress of the house to assist and

*The nursery in Ann Sharp's Baby House. A miniature baby house made from paper stands to the right of a fine walnut cradle, inlaid with ivory. (Private collection: photograph by N. Nicholson)*

*Some miniature toys from Ann Sharp's Baby House. There is a miniature dolls' house in the nursery. Most of the contents of this house were made by hand although it would have been possible to buy them from suppliers. (Private collection: photograph by N. Nicholson)*

supervise the kitchen staff but gradually these duties came to be handed over to the housekeeper so that the mistress had more time to spend on her own pursuits and in receiving guests.

Possibly the most impressive of the great baby houses is in the care of the National Trust at Nostell Priory near Wakefield in West Yorkshire. It is thought that the baby house (1735–40) was probably made for the children of Sir Rowland Winn and Susanne Henshaw, who had married in 1729.

It was designed by the architect James Paine and is loosely based on the real Nostell Priory. The magnificently crafted doors slide into position together and great care has been paid to detail throughout. It is believed that the period furniture may well have been made by Thomas Chippendale, who organised the furnishing of the real Nostell Priory for Sir Rowland Winn

*The Uppark Baby House from West Sussex (1730–40). Each of the nine rooms can be opened by its own door. (National Trust Photographic Library)*

*The withdrawing room of the Nostell Priory Baby House (1735–40). Rich yellow paper decorated with pastoral scenes gives this room an air of elegant luxury. (National Trust Photographic Library)*

Below left: *The Nostell Priory Baby House, West Yorkshire; tradition has it that the furniture in this splendid baby house may have been designed by Thomas Chippendale. (National Trust Photographic Library: photograph by Andreas von Einsiedel)*

Below right: *A winding staircase in a baby house made about 1730. There is a door to the side of the stairs, behind which is a cupboard. The winding stairs do not lead to an upper landing. (Mark and Marjorie Allen Antiques: photograph courtesy of Bonhams)*

*A well stocked kitchen in an eighteenth-century house. Many of the pieces are good-quality later additions. Despite this, the kitchen has the air of an earlier room. (Private collection: photograph by John Gould)*

*The bedroom in the same eighteenth-century house. Note the chairs made by Evans & Cartwright, who made tin-plate dolls' house furniture c.1800–80. (Private collection: photograph by John Gould)*

*Left: The Van Haeften House (1740–50). The house has a fine Palladian exterior and sits on an arched base. (Mark and Marjorie Allen Antiques: photograph courtesy of Bonhams)*

between 1766 and 1776. The dolls representing the family are made of wax and the servants of wood, following the custom of the time.

This house also consists of nine rooms arranged on three levels. The furniture for each level is made of a different material: oak, walnut and ivory. The family would have dined in the great hall (as in the Sharp household). The lying-in room (on the top floor) was as important a feature of English life as it was on the continent and was expected to be an attractive reception room with a welcoming atmosphere. The wet nurse is present in the room; most wealthy ladies paid large sums of money to nursing women to feed their babies. All the details of the interior are perfect replicas, from the miniature marble chimney-pieces to the working locks and handles on the doors.

A grand double staircase leads up to the entrance of the Blackett Baby House (1740) in the Museum of London. It has hand-painted wallpaper and retains its original festooned curtains and original occupants.

Another grand house is on display at the Bethnal Green Museum of Childhood. The Tate Baby House (*c.*1760) was made in Dorset and is supposedly modelled on an eighteenth-century Dorset house. It is a complex structure because it is composed of

*The interior of the Van Haeften House (1740–50). Fortunately this has not been 'improved' and retains original architectural details such as the panelling, the shelving and fireplace in the kitchen and two surviving pictures above the mantelpiece. (Mark and Marjorie Allen Antiques: photograph courtesy of Bonhams)*

*This house, which dates from about 1740, is known as the King's Lynn Baby House. It was identified in 1984 as a miniature of a real house in King's Lynn, Norfolk. The little house had been made for the daughter of a Dutch merchant who lived there. Vivien Greene restored the house, of which only the original panelling, door and fireplaces had survived. (Town House Museum of Lynn Life: photograph by N. Nicholson)*

three sections which separate to make it easier to transport. The house is on three levels and is supported on a solid stand. The dining room and parlour are on the central level, accessible from the courtyard by a sweeping main staircase. Unfortunately the glazing bars on the windows have been lost; the windows would have had an authentic twelve-paned appearance instead of the two-paned sash windows that were fashionable in the nineteenth century. The contents of the house were revised in 1830 and there are several obvious later additions.

The King's Lynn Baby House, now at the Town House Museum of Lynn Life in King's Lynn, Norfolk, has a fascinating history. It was presented to a children's home in Torquay run by the Children's Society in the 1920s. It was restored in 1984 and furnished with furniture appropriate to the period of the house (*c*.1740). The house, which is set on an arched base, was found to be a replica in miniature, except for its balustrade, of an actual house in King's Lynn. It had been made for Ann Flierden, the daughter of a Dutch merchant, who had lived in the house.

These magnificent English baby houses were furnished with mainly expensive items mingled with cheap toys. Dolls' houses and furniture for them were certainly available commercially in the eighteenth century from shops such as Bellamy's of Holborn and Hamleys, which was established in 1760. It is likely that the principal purpose of these houses was to serve as expensive amusements for adults. Children would have been permitted to play with them, probably under strict supervision on special occasions. The high standard of craftsmanship that went into making and furnishing them has seldom been surpassed since.

Above left: *This is a delightful example of a small eighteenth-century baby house probably made for travelling. The green curtains at the windows are painted in. It is made of mahogany and decorated at roof level with an ivory and mother-of-pearl lozenge and two brass balls. (Tara's Palace Trust, Malahide Castle, Dublin: photograph courtesy of Bonhams)*

Above right: *This house dates from the latter part of the eighteenth century and has the look of a town house. Dolls' houses had by this time started to resemble the small buildings which were made in large numbers in the nineteenth century. This house is known as Farnham House. (Private collection: photograph courtesy of Bonhams)*

Below: *The front of a late-eighteenth-century house. Unfortunately the decorative detail is missing from the lower left-hand window. (Private collection: photograph by John Gould)*

Left: *The same late-eighteenth-century house. The front drops down to reveal four elegant rooms furnished with furniture from a later period. (Private collection: photograph by John Gould)*

24

# The dolls' house in the nineteenth century

During the nineteenth century the expansion of industry and commerce provided opportunities for more people to acquire wealth through their talents rather than their social status. The possession of wealth produced a demand for comfortable homes equipped with labour-saving devices and amenities made possible by developments in technology. The dolls' houses of the period reflect those technological changes to some extent. German toy manufacturers, such as Eduard and Louis Lindner of Sonneberg (c.1840–2), began to advertise their wares by producing sample sheets depicting the available merchandise, including dolls' houses. Toys were also provided by British toymakers, who used their families as workers in the manufacture of objects that, because of their cheapness, were hardly ever durable. There was a wide choice of furniture, from hand-made items fashioned from wishbones and feathers to articles made from brass, copper, tin, earthenware and pewter; these had superseded the expensive ivory, silver, alabaster and lignum-vitae from which the miniature utensils of the previous two centuries had been made.

*The magnificent exterior of Compton Chamberlayne, built in 1881 by Edward Towry White of Carlisle (1847–1932), architect and craftsman, who later lived in Compton Chamberlayne, Wiltshire. (Michal Morse Collection)*

Many solidly built houses have fortunately survived and the Bethnal Green Museum of Childhood has a large number on display, of which Amy Miles's House is a particularly good

*Exterior and interior views of the Longleat Dolls' House, made in about 1870 for the three daughters of the fourth Marquess of Bath by the estate carpenter. This is a model of a house at Abbeyleix, County Laois, Ireland, which belonged to the girls' grandfather, Lord de Vesci. (By kind permission of the Marquess of Bath, Longleat: photographs by Lord Christopher Thynne)*

Right: 'No 12' is painted on the door of this house, which has therefore subsequently become known as 'No 12'. It is of the type known as box-back (flat backed) and may be of German or English origin, dating from the 1870s. Like many other large dolls' houses made in the style of town houses, the plain exterior belies the sumptuous and comfortable interior. (Faith Eaton Collection: photograph by John Gould)

Below: A chair made from a wishbone in the nineteenth century, now part of the furniture of the late-eighteenth-century house on page 24. A rare example of a toy made from scrap materials. (Private collection: photograph by John Gould)

example. This house, which was made in the 1890s, contains a carpet-sweeper, a telephone, a bicycle and a water-heater, amongst many other contemporary labour-saving items. The bathroom and hall walls are covered in sanitary paper to make them completely authentic. Sanitary wallpaper was varnished to make it washable and was used in halls, bathrooms, sculleries and other areas in the home that were likely to get damp.

Nineteenth-century dolls' houses have an air of comfort

Amy Miles's House, 1890s, in the Bethnal Green Museum of Childhood. This house contains many examples of labour-saving devices introduced during the nineteenth century. (Courtesy of the V&A Picture Library)

and prosperity about them. They look more like large town houses than vast country mansions and many more families were able to afford them either for themselves or for their children. However, large houses were still status symbols; the Hammond House at Wallington Hall in Northumberland is a delightful example of the transition from elegant baby house to the commercially produced toy of the late eighteenth century. The house itself is fairly crudely constructed, consisting of thirty-six rooms linked by corridors. As in Amy Miles's House the fascination lies in the fittings and contents: there is a lift and electric lighting and a huge team of servants to deal with the many demands that such a house would have presented. Hammond House originally had water piped from

*The room setting has been assembled by its owner to form this charming late-nineteenth-century scene with mother and new-born child receiving visitors. (Faith Eaton Collection: photograph by John Gould)*

the roof to the bathroom and scullery, a system which was then a marvel of technology. Unfortunately the pipes have since corroded.

At Audley End in Essex another vast dolls' house, somewhat crudely constructed between 1820 and 1840, contains an interesting mixture of home-made and shop-bought pieces, including some splendid pressed-tin furniture.

Houses such as these mirror the comfortable domestic lives of the well-to-do families of the nineteenth century. Humbler houses were also produced, such as Contented Cot made by Henry Hall, master mariner of Brixham, Devon. A note pasted inside the attic tells us that he made it to commemorate the birth of his

*We know the name and date of this welcoming little house because they appear on the building itself. The date 1886 is above the attic window and the name Contented Cot above the door. It was made by Henry Hall of Brixham, Devon, to celebrate the birth of his daughter. (Faith Eaton Collection: photograph by John Gould)*

daughter on 11th October 1886.

Queen Mary (1867–1953) was an avid collector of dolls' houses. The Museum of London has one of her houses in its collections. Another example at the Bethnal Green Museum of Childhood was made by Ashcroft, billiard-table makers of Liverpool, in 1887. Queen Mary bought the house and supervised the furnishing of it before giving it to the museum in 1921. In the drawing room are framed photographs of members of the Royal Family. The house featured in a special exhibition at the museum in the 1920s and was enthusiastically received by the press.

By the end of the nineteenth century the manufacture of dolls' houses was fully established as an industry in its own right. Several important makers were emerging. Rupert Bliss (1832–1914) of Pawtucket in the United States made small houses of wood embellished with lithographed paper and houses that could be folded away. Christian Hacker (c.1870–1914) of Nuremberg made beautiful houses with considerable decorative detail; much of his work was

Above left: *The Welsh House, 1860s, with four rooms and stairs. (Michal Morse Collection: photograph by Michal Morse)*

Above right: *This large dolls' house on a stand dates from about 1840. It was kept in the same Sussex family until 1987, when it was bought for Worthing Museum and Art Gallery. The house has six rooms, two attics and a separate kitchen, which was probably a later extension as it obscures the living-room window. (Courtesy of Worthing Museum and Art Gallery)*

formerly considered French because of its light and elegant style. Moritz Gottschalk (1865–1939) of Marienberg, Germany, was a major manufacturer of dolls' houses; he also used colour lithography to decorate his houses, which often resembled villas and romantic miniature castles. In England the Lines family, using the thistle trademark, had begun to make dolls' houses in the solid traditional style that was to make the firm so successful in the twentieth century.

Far left: *A French seaside villa of about 1880. Although this is a very simple house it would still have been regarded as a luxury toy by the average family.*

Left: *The interior of the French seaside villa with two rooms furnished in keeping with the period. A real home of the time would have been furnished similarly.*

*This grand house, which incorporates a mix of architectural styles, dates from about 1905. It opens on both sides, has thirteen rooms and a conservatory. (Private collection: photograph by N. Nicholson)*

# The dolls' house after 1900

*Below left: An attractive house, probably made in Germany in about 1913. It has lithographed bricks and side windows. A similar house was illustrated in Gamages' catalogue of the time. (Michal Morse Collection: photograph by Michal Morse)*

At the beginning of the twentieth century there was a growing awareness of the importance of good design in a child's environment, and particular attention was paid to nurseries and children's rooms. Artists such as Claud Lovat Fraser, Jessie Marion King and Roger Fry all designed dolls' houses. Roger Fry started the Omega Workshops in 1913 with the painters Duncan Grant and Vanessa Bell for the purpose of encouraging young artists to design and decorate everyday items in a bold, innovative style. He designed a dolls' house that was rectangular in shape with a plain exterior, said to have been based on his own house, Durbins, near Guildford. This was one of several toys made by the Omega Workshops and was similar to a dolls' house included in a design for an ideal nursery exhibited on the

*Seventh Heaven at Snowshill Manor, Gloucestershire, made by Charles Wade in about 1910 and furnished with nineteenth-century furniture. It is inhabited by Lord Mex and family. (National Trust Photographic Library: photograph by Andreas von Einsiedel)*

31

premises in 1913.

The legendary Titania's Palace, designed by the artist and writer Sir Nevile Wilkinson in 1907 for his daughter Gwendoline, travelled the world in the 1920s raising funds for underprivileged children. Britannia House was built by Kevin Mulvaney in the 1980s for the African Medical and Research Council. Designers such as Nina Campbell and Colefax & Fowler contributed individual decorative schemes for the rooms.

During the early twentieth century the commercial production of dolls' houses increased considerably. Until then Britain had imported large numbers of toys from Germany but the introduction of high import duties on large items reduced the quantity and the outbreak of war in 1914 put an end to trading relations during the hostilities.

After the war small firms were set up to make toys, partly to provide work for ex-servicemen. Lord Roberts Memorial Workshops (1899 to c.1923), which had made furniture, began manufacturing different types of product. Of the commercial companies probably the most famous was Lines Brothers Limited, founded in 1919 and now represented by the triangular trademark that symbolised the partnership of the three brothers. The dolls' houses produced by the Lines family were well constructed miniature replicas of the type of house being built in the suburbs. The styles changed little because of their popularity, so that houses in mock Tudor, Queen Anne and thatched cottage styles continued to be produced until well into the century. Lines kept pace with the times by producing a small number of houses that reflected contemporary movements in architecture, such as the plain geometric houses of the 1920s and 1930s. They made houses to suit almost all pockets. Additional features such as plumbing and electricity were available at extra cost and even a repair and redecoration service was available for houses that they had made.

However, whilst Lines Brothers and other less well-known firms continued to manufacture houses of a traditional nature,

A fretwork house dating from the 1920s and made from commercial plans. It has five rooms, stairs, balconies and widow's walk. It also has facilities for running water, with taps, and a pressure pump in the attic. (Michal Morse Collection: photograph by Michal Morse)

Left: *A dolls' house made by Lines Brothers in the 1930s, on display in the Vina Cooke Museum of Dolls and Bygone Childhood. Although dolls' houses in the traditional suburban style continued in popularity, Lines Brothers also produced a small number of contemporary houses. (Photograph by Norman Roberts)*

*A 1929 house made by Lines Brothers, bearing a Hamleys label. Lines Brothers produced a large range of houses that were mainly traditional in style. (Faith Eaton Collection: photograph by John Gould)*

*A house made by Lines Brothers in the 1930s, one of a popular range of dolls' houses with electric light fittings and fully opening metal windows. Houses like these were made for a long time, reflecting customers' taste for a traditional style. (Kim Philpot Collection: photograph by Kim Philpot)*

newer influences were making their mark on the history of the dolls' house, namely the concept of a house designed with the educational needs of the child in mind. Paul and Marjorie Abbatt opened a child-friendly shop in 1936 in Wimpole Street, London, designed by their friend the architect Erno Goldfinger in such a way that children were allowed to see and touch everything and to take part in the process of selection. The dolls' houses sold there were simple structures with lift-off roofs and open sides to allow for maximum manoeuvrability and imaginative play. Paul Abbatt wrote in *Play and Toys*: 'Their hands must have easy

Above left: *A house designed to encourage imaginative play. It is simple but solid, made from easily found materials, the wood being natural and unpainted. It can be taken apart and reassembled as the child wishes. It was designed by Jane Blythe, an architectural student, in about 1970. (Faith Eaton Collection: photograph by John Gould)*

Above right: *A wooden dolls' house made by hand in 1955. This little house serves a useful purpose as part of a schools' loan pack. (The Cumberland Toy and Model Museum)*

access to the interior of the dolls' house so that they may arrange and rearrange the furniture and imagine themselves in charge of all domestic affairs.'

Another advantage of the open-sided house is that it can be used for group play in a nursery or playschool. A house of this type designed by Roger Limbrick for J. Galt won the *Observer* Design Award in 1969. It was a constructional kit consisting of nine pieces which when made up became a simple open house, and heralded a new type of dolls' house. Bodo Hennig of Germany makes high-quality flat-pack self-assembly houses from wood. The *Bambino* dolls' room offers a range of construction possibilities limited only by the child's imagination. The Second World War (1939–45) brought with it many

*Some of the Bambino range of dolls' house furniture designed for small children by Bodo Hennig. Made from maple, it is finely sanded but not treated; paint and other decorative features are non-toxic. (Bodo Hennig)*

*The Bambino-Combi, a sturdy dolls' house for small children. This house was made to be played with by nursery groups as well as individual children. It is made from pine by Bodo Hennig of Germany, who also manufactures safe, attractive and strong contemporary dolls' house furniture. (Bodo Hennig)*

*The Piccola dolls' house with removal vans, which increase scope for role play and creativity. This house, which comes as a self-assembly kit, was made for 2000 by Bodo Hennig of Germany for children from three years old. (Bodo Hennig)*

shortages. As wood was in short supply, tin and cardboard were used to make dolls' houses but more important than this was the greatly increased use of plastics in their manufacture. The popular Caroline's Home, introduced by Barton in 1957, continued to be produced by the Swedish firm Lundby after Barton sold out to them in 1984 and the famous dolls Barbie and Sindy each had their own homes, traditional in style and fully equipped with up-to-the-minute furniture. An element of fantasy was introduced in the 1980s with products such as the Bluebird Teapot House, the Sylvanian Families and their homes, and more recently the successful Polly Pocket range.

Making houses from kits has become a hugely popular hobby throughout the world. In England

*A small dolls' house made by hand in 1942. It is made of wood and is equipped with a battery light in each room. Toys made during the Second World War tended to be simple and solid. (The Cumberland Toy and Model Museum)*

Left: *Two rooms by Lundby of Sweden of the 1970s containing good-quality, contemporary miniature furniture from a range of materials including plastics, wood and metal. (Faith Eaton Collection: photograph by John Gould)*

Right: *Caroline's Home, a brightly coloured, vivid and attractive open-access home. Barton introduced this to the firm's range in 1957 and it quickly became popular. In 1984 Barton sold out to the famous Swedish firm Lundby, which carried on making Caroline's Home. (Faith Eaton Collection: photograph by John Gould)*

Left: *The Barbie Family House, 2000, a new home for the third millennium for the famous doll, made by Mattel UK Ltd. (Courtesy of Mattel UK)*

Right: *A house by Lundby of Sweden, complete with furniture and occupants. (Courtesy of Brian Meade Agencies for Lundby)*

Above: *The Playmobil House made by the Brand-statter Company in 1989 with furniture and spacious and comfortable interiors designed by Geobra Brandstatter. The colourful and sturdy furniture is of non-toxic plastic. (Playmobil UK Ltd, in the Faith Eaton Collection: photograph by John Gould)*

Right: *The Playmobil House is made of non-toxic plastic. Its architectural style is very similar to that of the early 1900s. It has a splendid conservatory. (Playmobil UK Ltd, in the Faith Eaton Collection: photograph by John Gould)*

Left: *A tin-plate dolls' house made by Mettoy in the 1950s. After the war the use of metal in the manufacture of dolls' houses greatly increased. In the USA lithographed tin-plate buildings were being produced as early as 1869. (Vina Cooke Museum of Dolls and Bygone Childhood: photograph by Norman Roberts)*

Right: *This house was hand-made by its owner following instructions in a book published by the American School of Needlework. It took a year to sew and put together and is made from plastic canvas with beads, mirror card, curtain rings and channel pipes. (Kim Philpot Collection: photograph by Kim Philpot)*

there are several firms selling kits, one of the best-known of which is the Dolls' House Emporium in Ripley, Derbyshire. For the year 2000 they designed and produced in kit form a model of a house in the style of Charles Rennie Mackintosh, an innovative addition to their range. The making and furnishing of dolls' houses is still as absorbing a pastime as it has ever been for child and adult alike.

The most spectacular house of the

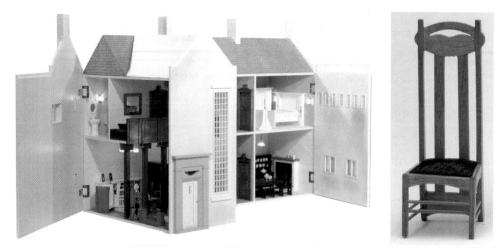

Above left: *A house in the style of the great Scottish architect Charles Rennie Mackintosh (1868–1928), whose simple and uncluttered style became well-known all over the world and provided a complete contrast to the cosy and dark domestic interiors of the period. The Dolls' House Emporium produced this two-storey house with three opening panels, together with exquisite furniture and fittings, as a tribute to the architect and to mark the millennium year, 2000. (Courtesy of the Dolls' House Emporium)*

Above right: *A miniature dining chair, a replica of a real chair designed for the Argyle Street Tea Rooms in Glasgow in 1897, one of Charles Rennie Mackintosh's most famous designs. (Courtesy of the Dolls' House Emporium)*

twentieth century was the one built in the 1920s for Queen Mary by Sir Edwin Lutyens and exhibited at the British Empire Exhibition at Wembley in 1924. Intended as a token of affection for the Queen, almost every item was funded by gifts and donations and virtually all the contents were specially commissioned, including seven hundred tiny drawings and paintings by well-known artists of the time. Even the drawers under the house pull out to reveal a garden designed by Gertrude Jekyll and a garage full of miniature versions of the best British-made cars. It is an interesting coincidence that this magnificent house should have so much in common with that first recorded house made for Albert V of Bavaria in the sixteenth century.

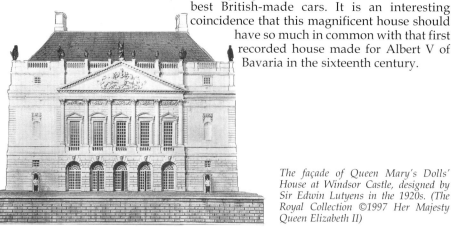

*The façade of Queen Mary's Dolls' House at Windsor Castle, designed by Sir Edwin Lutyens in the 1920s. (The Royal Collection ©1997 Her Majesty Queen Elizabeth II)*

# Further reading

Baker, Roger. *Dolls and Dolls' Houses*. Orbis Books, 1973.
Bristol, Olivia, and Geddes-Brown, Leslie. *Dolls' Houses*. Mitchell Beazley, 1997.
Clifton-Mogg, Caroline. *The Dolls' House Sourcebook*. Cassell, 1993.
Earnshaw, Nora. *Collecting Dolls' Houses and Miniatures*. Collins, 1989.
Eaton, Faith. *The Miniature House*. Weidenfeld & Nicolson, 1990.
Eaton, Faith. *The Ultimate Dolls' House Book*. Dorling Kindersley, 1994.
Flick, Pauline. *The Dolls' House Book*. Collins, 1973.
Glubok, Shirley. *Dolls' Houses: Life in Miniature*. Harper & Row, New York, 1984.
Greene, Vivien. *English Dolls' Houses of the 18th and 19th Centuries*. B. T. Batsford, 1955;
    reprinted by Bell & Hyman, 1979.
Greene, Vivien. *The Dolls' House in Scotland 1800 to the Present Day*. Academy Editions, 1982.
Greene, Vivien, and Towner, Margaret. *The Vivien Greene Dolls' House Collection*. Cassell, 1995.
Jackson, Valerie. *Dolls' Houses and Miniatures*. John Murray, 1988.
King, Constance E. *The Collectors' History of Dolls' Houses, Dolls' House Dolls and Miniatures*.
    Robert Hale, 1983.
Latham, Jean. *Dolls' Houses*. Adam & Charles Black, 1969.
Pasierbska, Halina. *Dolls' House Furniture*. Shire, 1998.
Stille, Eva. *Doll Kitchens 1800–1980*. Schiffer Publishing, 1988.
Towner, Margaret. *Dolls' House Furniture*. The Apple Press, 1993.
Wilckens, L. von. *The Dolls' House: An Illustrated History*. Bell & Hyman, 1980.
Wilson, Mary S. *Queen Mary's Dolls' House*. Bodley Head, 1988.

PERIODICALS
*Dolls' House and Miniature Scene*, The Old Barn, Ferringham Lane, Ferring, West Sussex
    BN12 5LL. Telephone: 01903 244900.
*Dolls' House Magazine*, GMC Publications Ltd, 166 High Street, Lewes, East Sussex BN7 1XU.
    Telephone: 01273 488005.
*Dolls' House World*, Avalon Court, Star Road, Partridge Green, West Sussex RH13 8RY.
    Telephone: 01403 711511.
*International Dolls' House News*, Avalon Court, Star Road, Partridge Green, West Sussex
    RH13 8RY. Telephone: 01403 711511.

CATALOGUES
*The Dolls' House Emporium* (see pages 37 and 38): colour catalogue available from The Dolls'
House Emporium, EDI, High Holborn Road, Ripley, Derbyshire DE5 3YD. Telephone:
01773 514400. Website: www.dollshouse.co.uk

*The Dolls' House*, Market Place, Northleach,
Gloucestershire GL54 3EJ. Telephone/fax: 01451
860431.

*The kitchen in 'Mon Plaisir', an eighteenth-century German dolls' house made for Princess Augusta Dorothea of Schwarzburg-Arnstadt (see pages 4–5). (Museen der Stadt, Arnstadt: photograph by N. Nicholson)*

# Places to visit

Dolls' houses may be seen at the following places. However, before travelling, readers are advised to check dates and times of opening and also to confirm that the dolls' houses will be on display.

*Abbey House Museum*, Abbey Road, Kirkstall, Leeds LS5 3EH. Telephone: 0113 230 5492.
*Audley End House*, Saffron Walden, Essex CB11 4JF. Telephone: 01799 522842.
*Bethnal Green Museum of Childhood*, Cambridge Heath Road, London E2 9PA. Telephone: 020 8983 5212. Website: www.museumofchildhood.org.uk
*The Bowes Museum*, Barnard Castle, County Durham DL12 8NP. Telephone: 01833 690606. Website: www.durham.gov.uk/bowes
*Cumberland Toy and Model Museum*, Banks Court, Market Place, Cockermouth, Cumbria CA13 9NG. Telephone: 01900 827606.
*House on the Hill Toy Museum*, Stansted, Essex CM24 8SP. Telephone: 01279 813567.
*Hove Museum and Art Gallery*, 19 New Church Road, Hove, East Sussex BN3 4AB. Telephone: 01273 290200. Website: www.brighton-hove.gov.uk
*Judges' Lodgings*, Church Street, Lancaster LA1 1YS. Telephone: 01524 846315.
*Longleat House*, Warminster, Wiltshire BA12 7NW. Telephone: 01985 844400. Website: www.longleat.co.uk
*Museum of Childhood*, 42 High Street, Edinburgh EH1 1TG. Telephone: 0131 529 4142.
*Museum of Childhood Memories*, 1 Castle Street, Beaumaris, Isle of Anglesey LL58 8AP. Telephone: 01248 712498. Website: www.nwi.co.uk/museumofchildhood
*Museum of London*, London Wall, London EC2Y 5HN. Telephone: 020 7600 3699. Website: www.museum-london.org.uk (Large collection in store viewable by appointment only.)
*National Trust Sudbury Hall and the Museum of Childhood*, Sudbury Hall, Sudbury, Ashbourne, Derbyshire DE6 5HT. Telephone: 01283 585305.
*Nostell Priory*, Doncaster Road, Wakefield, West Yorkshire WF4 1QE. Telephone: 01924 863892.
*Nunnington Hall*, Nunnington, North Yorkshire YO62 5UY. Telephone: 01439 748283. Website: www.nationaltrust.org.uk
*Penrhyn Castle*, Bangor, Gwynedd LL57 4HN. Telephone: 01248 353084. Website: www.nationaltrust.org.uk
*Penshurst Place and Gardens*, Tonbridge, Kent TN11 8DG. Telephone: 01892 870307. Website: www.penshurstplace.com
*Pollock's Toy Museum*, 1 Scala Street, London W1P 1LT. Telephone: 020 7636 3452. Website: www.pollocks.cwc.net
*Strangers' Hall Museum*, Charing Cross, Norwich, Norfolk NR2 4AL. Telephone: 01603 667229 (by appointment only). Website: www.norfolk.gov.uk/tourism/museums
*Tara's Palace Trust,* Malahide Castle, Malahide Demesne, County Dublin, Ireland.
*Town House Museum of Lynn Life*, 46 Queen Street, King's Lynn, Norfolk PE30 5DQ. Telephone: 01553 773450.
*Uppark*, South Harting, Petersfield, Hampshire GU31 5QR. Telephone: 01730 825415. Website: www.nationaltrust.org.uk/regions/southern
*Vina Cooke Museum of Dolls and Bygone Childhood*, The Old Rectory, Cromwell, Newark, Nottinghamshire NG23 6JE. Telephone: 01636 821364.
*Wallington*, Cambo, Morpeth, Northumberland NE61 4AR. Telephone: 01670 774283.
*Wilton House*, Wilton, Salisbury, Wiltshire SP2 0BJ. Telephone: 01722 746720. Website: www.wiltonhouse.com
*Windsor Castle*, Windsor, Berkshire SL4 1NJ. Telephone: 01753 868286. Website: www.royal.gov.uk
*Worthing Museum and Art Gallery*, Chapel Road, Worthing, West Sussex BN11 1HP. Telephone: 01903 239999.
*York Castle Museum*, Eye of York, York YO1 9RY. Telephone: 01904 653611. Website: www.york.gov.uk